JAZZ ESSENTIALS

"NUTS & BOLTS" INSTRUCTION FOR THE JAZZ & POP MUSICIAN

BY KELLY DEAN

ILLUSTRATIONS BY TODD HARRISON

ISBN 0-7935-4254-5

HAL•LEONARD®
CORPORATION
7777 W. BLUEMOUND RD. P.O. BOX 13819 MILWAUKEE, WI 53213

Visit Hal Leonard Online at
www.halleonard.com

Table of Contents

Outcomes

By the end of this book, you will have accomplished the following:

1. Memorized the names of all the notes on the piano (including enharmonic spellings).

2. Learned to spell Major scales in all 15 keys (up to 7 ♯s and ♭s).

3. Learned to spell major, minor, augmented and diminished triads in all keys.

4. Learned to spell major, minor, dominant, half-diminished, and diminished 7th chords in all keys.

5. Learned the names and structures of **the big five** scales in all keys.

6. Learned how to read (and write) chord changes and figure out what to do with them.

7. Learned the secret superpowers of the major scale.

8. Identified intervals, and know the distinction between enharmonic equivalents.

9. Learned the basic concepts of improvisation.

10. Found out what's hip in the jazz bin of your CD store.

11. Learned what to do when you've finished this book.

12. Learned the name of a really good pizza place in Moline, IL.

Acknowledgements

There is no such thing as a self-made musician. Even if a musician *were* capable of sitting around and figuring all this stuff out without books, CDs, instructors, or fellow musicians (pretty unlikely scenario), there's still the problem of food; somebody has to be getting sponged on!

The CDs listed in chapter 9 are only a tiny portion of the influential music that I've listened to these many years. I'll listen to a recording I haven't heard in awhile, and find that I quoted from a solo the night before, without realizing it! The musicians mentioned have been key in helping me construct (or destruct) my life philosophy. To that list I would include Stevie Wonder, who made me understand through his music how blessed I've been, and how important it is to look beyond mere pigmentation.

I was fortunate to attend middle school when there was a window of opportunity to study jazz music (in public school!) almost from the moment I picked up a horn. My San Antonio instructors (Larry Schmidt, the Esquivel Brothers, Joe Freilich) did a great job of planting the seeds. I would have to say, though, that my most profound influence in the classroom was Curt Bradshaw at the Arts Magnet High School in Dallas. From dominant 7th chords to the overtone series, Curt drilled it all into us. Some of what he taught took years to soak in, which in some ways is the best kind of teacher: time-released!

I've worked with (and against) hundreds of musicians. Some have been an inspiration in music ("Wow, I hope I can play like *him* someday!") or in life ("Wow, I hope I don't end up like *him* someday!"). I feel lucky, though, that the best musicians I've ever worked with are the Houston players I've met in the last four years. Particularly, I'd like to thank Warren Sneed,

Mark Holter, Noe Marmolejo, Claudia Burson, Todd Harrison, Dave Foster, Joel Fulgham, and Kerry Movassagh for their contributions to the amazing "desert island" collection in Chapter 9. The music they suggested (and the music that they play) gives me the strength and desire to stay in "the shed" just a little longer.

My thanks to the former and current members of the Portsmouth Club–Rhonda Dean, Patrick Davis, Jason Whitmore, Jay Hendrickson, and Todd Harrison–for technical assistance, free meals, support and encouragement, and the ability to knock the wind out of my sails when I get a little carried away. Rhonda is "Mrs. Kel" and were it not for her, I'd still be stuck in "rewritesville." Thanks to Rhonda, I've managed to "run it up the flagpole and see if anybody salutes." She's also helped me keep my cool whenever the hard drive "abort, re-try, ignore, fail'ed" me! And now with the arrival of "Baby Kel," I have a whole new source of inspiration!

Even without all of that, I might still have been able to do all right. But I never realized until college just how fortunate I was to be a part of the family I was in. To my bros, David and Andrew: Dave for writing a really big book (dissertation), inspiring me to "whip a little something up myself". And Andy for keeping me from getting too analytical ("I don't care what you call that scale…it still sucks! Play something I can *feel!*"). Both of my brothers are responsible for dragging me into the 20th century, introducing me to computers, and not giving me too much static whenever I'd format my program disk!

My Ft. Worth side of the family has always expressed pride and support in all my endeavors. I wish I was in Ft. Worth more often. My Houston side of the family has always felt like home. My great-Aunt Teet and Uncle Jack and Aunt Sally have always had nothing but positive things to say about my career choices. My Houston grandparents, George and Mary, have always been the "entertainment committee" — George taking the podium, telling jokes and beating up on Republicans, with Mary providing overflowing trays of food. Mary has provided additional inspiration by producing her own cookbook, forcing me to "publish or perish". Both have been big fans of mine, and their adulation has helped me set ever higher goals for myself.

Here's to the two that created this mess! Joe and Molly Dean have both been involved in teaching for the last few years. Their pupils have learned what my brothers and I have known all along: they care. They help, but don't get in the way. They support, but offer advice when asked. They encourage, and never nag. In short, they love. I'm eternally grateful. This one's for you, Mom and Dad!

Finally, I'd like to thank my students. Without them, this book would be a pointless waste of time. It was their thirst for knowledge that compelled me to tackle this project. It is my hope that this book will help them climb a little faster up the ladder of their musical training.

Introduction

Some will say it before they even open this book — "We need another music theory book like we need another daytime talk show!" Why discuss a topic that has already filled libraries with textbooks, periodicals, and dissertations? Because this book attempts to bridge the gap between music theory and music **reality.** The working musician may enjoy pontificating on the use of stretto in an isorhythmic motet (well, probably not), but what he **needs** is the scale B.B. King uses in "The Thrill Is Gone."

This book deals with the nuts and bolts of music. There's nothing glamorous about a pipe wrench, but nothing does the job quite like it! In music, students often are force-fed scales, without ever really being told why these scales are important. The key to this is the relation between scales and chords, both of which you will have a working knowledge of by the end of this book.

This book is **not** a substitute for real-time playing with human interfaces (un-geek translation: jamming with other musicians). If you memorize all this information, and then try "connecting the dots" with a band, your playing will resemble that of R2D2: interesting, in an academic-disconnected-from-reality-living-somewhere-in-the-middle-ages kind of a groove, but probably not what the guys at Moe's Tavern wanna hear.

In spite of this, there is a lot you *can* do at home, armed with nothing but this book and a well sharpened pencil.

What's 8 times 8? How about 9 times 7? Hopefully you said 64 and 63, in that order (if not, it may be time to dust off those multiplication tables!). How did you know the answer?

"Why," you say, "by memorization, of course." Well, much of music theory is set up in a logical framework that makes it easy to use tables of formulae (sorry, but I've always wanted to use that word in a sentence!). For instance, a half-diminished chord is always 1-♭3-♭5-♭7. If you know that, just plug in the necessary information and **presto**!! One perfectly good half-diminished chord!

"But wait," you say. "I don't know what a half-diminished chord is, or what 1-♭3-♭5-♭7 means!" Well, you need to read the first few chapters. This brings up an important aspect of utilizing this book. If you've had some background in music already, simply skim through until you find something useful. If you've never played an instrument or studied anything (about music!), then start from the beginning, and we'll walk it through.

While there is a lot that can be learned on paper, your learning will be enhanced by playing what you learn on an instrument. The best instrument to start on is a keyboard, because you have a graphic display of your digital excursion (you can **see** what you're doing!). If you live in an apartment, or have a high-strung roommate, an electronic keyboard of some kind will probably be preferable. Make sure it has a headphone jack, decent sounds, and full-sized keys (optional, but helpful in avoiding cramped hands).

If your instrument choice is a monophonic sound source (it can only play one note at a time), such as trumpet, sax or clarinet, you can still take advantage of your new-found knowledge, but it won't be visually advantageous (you **won't** be able to **see** what you're doing). Make sure that you use a drawing of a keyboard to reinforce what you learn on your instrument of choice.

That's about it, really. I've gotta look up a few more four-syllable words so I can impress you, and then we'll get started. Let the beatings begin!

CHAPTER 1

Learn the names of the piano keys (in 10 minutes or less!)

Spelling can only be achieved by knowing the alphabet (I made that up...pretty good, huh?). It's important to learn your ABCs before trying to spell antidisestablishmentarianism (oww, typer's cramp!). The same can be applied to music.

ATTENTION: PAY CLOSE ATTENTION TO THIS CHAPTER OR THE OTHER STUFF WILL NOT MAKE SENSE!!

Behold the lowly keyboard:

First, notice the pattern of the black keys (set of three, pair, set of three, pair, etc.). Use these to find your way around.

1. Find a pair of black keys. The white key to the left of the black pair is **C**.

2. Find a group of three black keys. The white key to the left of the set of three black keys is **F**.

Here's what you know so far...

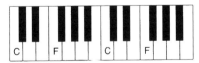

This pattern will continue the entire length of the keyboard.

3. If you know where C is, then the white key to the right must be D, and the white key to the left of it must be **B**.

4. If you know where **F** is, then the white key to the right must be G, and the white key to the left of it must be **E**.

The story so far...

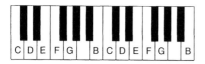

5. The musical alphabet only uses seven letters. Therefore, the note in between G and B has got to be **A**.

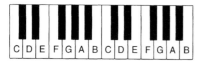

MAKE SURE YOU HAVE THESE KEYS FIRM IN YOUR MIND BEFORE CONTINUING WITH THE BOOK!!!

Yeah, the title of the chapter says under 10 minutes, but a little extra time spent right now will only do you good. Look for patterns for the other keys, like "D is in between the pair" or "B is just right of the group of three."

6. Music theory rule:

A sharp (♯) raises a note one half step. On the keyboard, this means the next available note up (to the right), including black keys.

At this point, some of you more observant folks may have noticed that this rule would seem to run into trouble between B-C or E-F, since these notes don't have black keys separating them. Not to worry, though...here's how it all ends up:

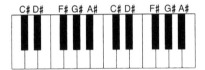

As you can see, a B♯ is just another name for C, and E♯ is another name for F.

7. More music theory:

A flat (♭) lowers a note one half step. On the keyboard, this means the next available note down (to the left), including black keys.

Second verse, same as the first.

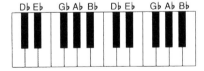

So, an F♭ is another name for E, and a C♭ is another name for B. These various names are known in "theory talk" as **enharmonic equivalents**.

B♯	= C	E♯	= F	A♯	= B♭		
C♯	= D♭	F♯	= G♭	F♭	= E		
D♯	= E♭	G♯	= A♭	C♭	= B		

Sharps and flats are sometimes referred to as **accidentals**. To cancel a sharp or flat, use a natural sign (♮).

If you try to read published music, you'll see the ♮ occasionally.

Spend a few minutes now to review this chapter. Practice guessing the names of the notes on the keyboard, and check back in the book often to make certain you are on the right track. Make certain you understand all of this before going on.

CHAPTER 2

The major scale...theory scaffolding

In **Monty Python and the Holy Grail**, there's a touching scene between a father and his son. The father describes the disadvantages of swamp real estate. The main problem is one of foundation technology. Apparently, building contractors of the Middle Ages weren't able to take advantage of bell-bottom piers, or the perma-pile method (those are some foundation repair buzzwords you can use to impress your friends!). Anyhow, learning music theory without knowledge of major scales is a lot like building castles on swamp land.

AS WITH THE PREVIOUS CHAPTER, THE INFORMATION HERE IS CRUCIAL TO UNDERSTANDING FUTURE CHAPTERS.
READ CAREFULLY, KEMOSABE!!

The major scale was used as the topic of a song in **The Sound Of Music** (remember Doe, a deer…etc). Well, in addition to being a star vehicle to launch Julie Andrews's career, the lowly major scale can also be used as the basis of understanding all music theory. The rest of this book will continuously make references to the major scale when dealing with more advanced concepts.

So, what about this here major scale? It's quite simple, really. The structure of the major scale looks like this:

```
1        2        3         4        5        6        7        8
└1 STEP┘ └1 STEP┘ └1/2 STEP┘ └1 STEP┘ └1 STEP┘ └1 STEP┘ └1/2 STEP┘
```

Looks like something out of chemistry class, right? The simple definition of a major scale in ten words or less is:

ONE STEP BETWEEN EACH NOTE, EXCEPT BETWEEN 3-4 AND 7-8

O.K., so it's 12 words if you count the numbers (14 if you count hyphens!).

One word now about **steps: A step is defined as an interval between two notes, wherein a leap has occurred over a third party. The resulting interval will be considered a binding contract. All rights reserved. Habeas Corpus. E Pluribus Unum.**

Yeeoww! Attorney talk!! Now that you're ready for a good lawsuit, go back to the keyboard (remember, way back in Chapter 1!).

Notice that when you go from C to D, you skip a key (C♯/D♭). This means that the interval between C and D is one step, also known as a whole step (also known as a major 2nd, but that's for *another* chapter!).

Now, try going from B to C. You don't skip anything, right? So, the interval between B and C is 1/2 a step, or a half step (or a minor second…oops, wrong chapter again!).

How about F to F♯? No skip, so half step. F♯ to G♯? Skip over G, so whole step. No problemo.

Now that you comprendo half steps and whole steps, there's one more thing to remember. The major scale is a seven-note scale (the eighth note will be a repeat of the first note). Since there are seven letters in the musical alphabet, you will need to use all seven letters when you are building the scale.

DON'T SKIP A LETTER, AND DON'T USE A LETTER TWICE.

It's time to do some scale construction.
Put on a hardhat and grab a welder!!

Start with **C**. The next letter is a whole step up,
so skip C♯, and grab **D**. 2 to 3 is a whole step,
so skip D♯ and take **E**. 3 to 4 is a half step,
so go from E to **F** (no skip). 4 to 5 is a whole step,
so skip F♯ and you land on **G**. 5 to 6 is a whole step,
so skip G♯ and get **A**. 6 to 7 is a whole step,
so skip A♯ and take **B**. Finally, 7 to 8 is a half step,
so B goes to **C**. Amazing! Here's what all that means:

```
  C         D         E         F         G         A         B         C
  ⌐1 STEP⌐ ⌐1 STEP⌐ ⌐1/2 STEP⌐ ⌐1 STEP⌐ ⌐1 STEP⌐ ⌐1 STEP⌐ ⌐1/2 STEP⌐
```

All right, maybe that was a little too easy. How about **C♯**? Well 1-2 is a whole step,
so skip D and go to **D♯**. 2-3 is a whole step, so skip E and go to **E♯**. 3-4 is a half step,
so go to **F♯**. 4-5 is a whole step, so skip G and go to **G♯**. 5-6 is a whole step, so skip A and
go to **A♯**. 6-7 is a whole step, so skip B and go to **B♯**. 7-8 is a half step,
so go straight to **C♯**. Unbelievable!!

```
  C♯        D♯        E♯        F♯        G♯        A♯        B♯        C♯
  ⌐1 STEP⌐ ⌐1 STEP⌐ ⌐1/2 STEP⌐ ⌐1 STEP⌐ ⌐1 STEP⌐ ⌐1 STEP⌐ ⌐1/2 STEP⌐
```

You can apply this formula to any starting note, and it will work. However, you may have to use double flats (♭♭) or double sharps (✕–not ♯♯!!) in order to follow the formula correctly. To avoid the double accidentals, leave out the following keys as starting notes:

D♯, E♯, G♯, A♯, B♯, F♭

But hey, that still leaves 15 keys to play with. So now, you have a choice. You can sneak a look at the next page, where all 15 scales are written out, or you can make a copy of the worksheet in Chapter 10, work the scales out for yourself, and check your answers with the next page.

Just how motivated are you?????

That's what I thought!!

20

MAJOR SCALES

C	D	E	F	G	A	B	C
C#	D#	E#	F#	G#	A#	B#	C#
D♭	E♭	F	G♭	A♭	B♭	C	D♭
D	E	F#	G	A	B	C#	D
E♭	F	G	A♭	B♭	C	D	E♭
E	F#	G#	A	B	C#	D#	E
F	G	A	B♭	C	D	E	F
F#	G#	A#	B	C#	D#	E#	F#
G♭	A♭	B♭	C♭	D♭	E♭	F	G♭
G	A	B	C	D	E	F#	G
A♭	B♭	C	D♭	E♭	F	G	A♭
A	B	C#	D	E	F#	G#	A
B♭	C	D	E♭	F	G	A	B♭
B	C#	D#	E	F#	G#	A#	B
C♭	D♭	E♭	F♭	G♭	A♭	B♭	C♭

CHAPTER 3

Triads...bricks of harmony

The information in this chapter can be learned without ever touching a keyboard…but it sounds much better if you do!

Triads are three-note chords. Several different sounding triads are available, depending on the structure that is used to build them. There are **four** common triads:

1. MAJOR TRIADS

This one's easy. Remember those pesky major scales? Now you have a new use for them (besides annoying your neighbors!). Simply take the 1st, 3rd, and 5th notes from a major scale, and you've built a major triad! **It's just that easy**.

Here's a real-life example. The first note of a C major scale is…that's right, **C**! The third note of the scale is **E**, and the fifth note is **G**. That's it! So a **C major triad** would be **C-E-G**. This works with any key, so all you have to do is find 1-3-5 in each major scale, and you've got all the major triads. Piece o' cake!!

2. MINOR TRIADS

Real simple. Just take the major triad and lower the 3rd by a half step. So, in **C**, a minor triad would be **C-E♭-G.**

3. AUGMENTED TRIADS

Again, no problemo. Find the major triad again and raise the 5th by a half step. In **C**, an augmented triad would be **C-E-G♯.**

4. DIMINISHED TRIADS

This one's a little tricky, but not too bad.
Take the major triad again, and this time
lower the 3rd **and** the 5th by one half step.
So, in C, a diminished triad would be **C-E♭-G♭**.

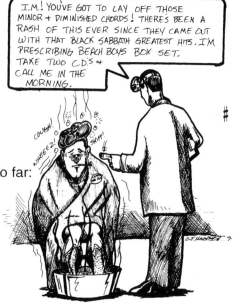

The following chart gives a summary of this chapter so far:

Type of Triad	Notes from Major Scale		
Major	1	- 3	- 5
Minor	1	- ♭3	- 5
Augmented	1	- 3	- #5
Diminished	1	- ♭3	- ♭5

Remember to keep the correct **enharmonic equivalent** when naming the notes. For instance, C-D#-G will sound correct as a minor triad on the keyboard, but the D# is enharmonically incorrect, because D is the second note of the C major scale, not the 3rd. The correct spelling would be C-E♭-G. Also, if you have a keyboard available, try playing the different triads. Soon you'll be able to tell the difference just by hearing them. Have a friend play the triads while you guess which of the four types is being played. Move around to different keys to make it more challenging.

You'll also start to hear these triads in the music on the radio, TV, or in your music collection. This is the beginning of **ear training**. Enjoy the discovery of being able to identify chord qualities just by **listening**.

Okay, okay, enough poetry. It's time to get back in the trenches. Chapter 10 has a chart you can copy and use to list all 4 triads in 15 keys. As with Chapter 2, you can work out the triads yourself using the worksheet, and then compare your answers with the chart at the end of this chapter. If you have a firm working knowledge of the major scales, triads are easy to build.

OTHER ACCIDENTALS

As you recall, sharps(♯) raise a note one half step, and flats lower a note one half step. Logically then, it's safe to assume that a double flat (♭♭) would lower a note two half steps (one whole step), and that a double sharp (✕) would raise it two half steps (one whole step). The purpose of the double sharp is to eliminate the possibility of having to constantly, for instance, go from G♯ to G (F✕). That's how it works **in theory**! In reality, an increase in the number of double accidentals in a piece of music will create a directly proportional increase in the blood pressure of a performing musician!! Jazz arrangers, in particular, go to unusual lengths to avoid them. In order to write triads enharmonically correct, however, it is sometimes necessary to use double accidentals. Below is a list of double accidental equivalents:

C✕ = D   D✕ = E   E✕ = F♯   F✕ = G   G✕ = A   A✕ = B   B✕ = C♯

C♭♭ = B♭   D♭♭ = C   E♭♭ = D   F♭♭ = E♭   G♭♭ = F   A♭♭ = G   B♭♭ = A

Here are a couple of examples of double accidentals in the triads. Take a B major triad. Remember that 1-3-5 in B is B-D♯-F♯. Now, in order to change a major triad to an augmented triad, you have to raise the 5th one half step. Since the 5th is an F♯, you have to add **another sharp** in order to raise the pitch. Therefore, a B augmented triad would be B-D♯-F✕.

Now, take a G♭ major triad (G♭-B♭-D♭) and change it to minor. Now, you need to lower the third (B♭) one more half step, so a G♭ minor triad would be G♭-B♭♭-D♭.

That's it. The chart below lists the four triads in 15 keys. To get a quick grasp on memorization, it's probably best to memorize the major triads first, and then just think of altering those triads to get the other three types. Also, look for the relationship between keys. For example, a G major triad is G-B-D, so a G♭ major triad has to be G♭-B♭-D♭. And you thought you'd never use algebra!!

TRIADS

KEY	MAJOR	MINOR	AUGMENTED	DIMINISHED
C	C - E - G	C - E♭ - G	C - E - G♯	C - E♭ - G♭
C♯	C♯ - E♯ - G♯	C♯ - E - G♯	C♯ - E♯ - G𝄪	C♯ - E - G
D♭	D♭ - F - A♭	D♭ - F♭ - A♭	D♭ - F - A	D♭ - F♭ - A♭♭
D	D - F♯ - A	D - F - A	D - F♯ - A♯	D - F - A♭
E♭	E♭ - G - B♭	E♭ - G♭ - B♭	E♭ - G - B	E♭ - G♭ - B♭♭
E	E - G♯ - B	E - G - B	E - G♯ - B♯	E - G - B♭
F	F - A - C	F - A♭ - C	F - A - C♯	F - A♭ - C♭
F♯	F♯ - A♯ - C♯	F♯ - A - C♯	F♯ - A♯ - C𝄪	F♯ - A - C
G♭	G♭ - B♭ - D♭	G♭ - B♭♭ - D♭	G♭ - B♭ - D	G♭ - B♭♭ - D♭♭
G	G - B - D	G - B♭ - D	G - B - D♯	G - B♭ - D♭
A♭	A♭ - C - E♭	A♭ - C♭ - E♭	A♭ - C - E	A♭ - C♭ - E♭♭
A	A - C♯ - E	A - C - E	A - C♯ - E♯	A - C - E♭
B♭	B♭ - D - F	B♭ - D♭ - F	B♭ - D - F♯	B♭ - D♭ - F♭
B	B - D♯ - F♯	B - D - F♯	B - D♯ - F𝄪	B - D - F
C♭	C♭ - E♭ - G♭	C♭ - E♭♭ - G♭	C♭ - E♭ - G	C♭ - E♭♭ - G♭♭

CHAPTER 4

7th chords...the big 5

Now that you understand triads, it's time to investigate the 7th chord possibilities. The 7th chords are going to have a denser sound, since they are **four-note** chords. This thicker sound is used often in modern music. While the sounds of triads have been used substantially in pop music, the slightly more dissonant 7th chords have been the primary chords of choice in jazz. There are five 7th chord families:

1. MAJOR 7TH CHORDS

This one's easy to remember. The major triad is 1-3-5, right? Well, the major 7th chord is **1-3-5-7**. So, in C, the major 7th chord would be **C-E-G-B**. That's it! No messy cleanup, no batteries to buy, no payments 'til next March!!!

2. DOMINANT 7TH CHORDS

Another simple, painless operation. Just take a major 7th chord, and lower the 7th one half step…**1-3-5-♭7**. So, a **C** dominant 7th chord would be **C-E-G-B♭**. This type of chord is sometimes referred to as a major-minor chord, because the triad is major and the 7th is minor. This is a dumb sounding name, though, and should only be used by overeducated people. In fact, **C-E-G-B♭** is referred to as simply "**C7**."

3. MINOR 7TH CHORDS

The simple definition of this chord is a minor triad with a minor (lowered) 7th. The formula is **1-♭3-5-♭7**. An example in **C** would be **C-E♭-G-B♭**. Not much else to say, really.

4. HALF-DIMINISHED CHORDS

This is just like a minor 7th chord, except that the 5th is lowered. For this reason, this chord is often referred to as "minor 7 ♭5." The formula is **1-♭3-♭5-♭7**. An example in C would be **C-E♭-G♭-B♭**. The triad is diminished, and the 7th is minor. Thus the name "half-diminished."

5. DIMINISHED CHORDS

Take a half-diminished chord, and lower the 7th another half step. This changes it from half-diminished to fully diminished. The formula is **1-♭3-♭5-♭♭7**. An example in C would be **C-E♭-G♭-B♭♭**.

Here's the good-'ol Chapter-at-a-glance:

Type of Seventh Chord	Notes from Major Scale
Major	1 - 3 - 5 - 7
Dominant	1 - 3 - 5 - ♭7
Minor	1 - ♭3 - 5 - ♭7
Half-Diminished	1 - ♭3 - ♭5 - ♭7
Diminished	1 - ♭3 - ♭5 - ♭♭7

Here are 7th chords in 15 keys. Use the blank chart in Chapter 10 to test yourself:

Key	Major	Dominant	Minor	Half-Diminished	Diminished
C	C - E - G - B	C - E - G - B♭	C - E♭ - G - B♭	C - E♭ - G♭ - B♭	C - E♭ - G♭ - B♭♭
C#	C# - E# - G# - B#	C# - E# - G# - B	C# - E - G# - B	C# - E - G - B	C# - E - G - B♭
D♭	D♭ - F - A♭ - C	D♭ - F - A♭ - C♭	D♭ - F♭ - A♭ - C♭	D♭ - F♭ - A♭♭ - C♭	D♭ - F♭ - A♭♭ - C♭♭
D	D - F# - A - C#	D - F# - A - C	D - F - A - C	D - F - A♭ - C	D - F - A♭ - C♭
Eb	E♭ - G - B♭ - D	E♭ - G - B♭ - D♭	E♭ - G♭ - B♭ - D♭	E♭ - G♭ - B♭♭ - D♭	E♭ - G♭ - B♭♭ - D♭♭
E	E - G# - B - D#	E - G# - B - D	E - G - B - D	E - G - B♭ - D	E - G - B♭ - D♭
F	F - A - C - E	F - A - C - E♭	F - A♭ - C - E♭	F - A♭ - C♭ - E♭	F - A♭ - C♭ - E♭♭
F#	F# - A# - C# - E#	F# - A# - C# - E	F# - A - C# - E	F# - A - C - E	F# - A - C - E♭
G♭	G♭ - B♭ - D♭ - F	G♭ - B♭ - D♭ - F♭	G♭ - B♭♭ - D♭ - F♭	G♭ - B♭♭ - D♭♭ - F♭	G♭ - B♭♭ - D♭♭ - F♭♭
G	G - B - D - F#	G - B - D - F	G - B♭ - D - F	G - B♭ - D♭ - F	G - B♭ - D♭ - F♭
A♭	A♭ - C - E♭ - G	A♭ - C - E♭ - G♭	A♭ - C♭ - E♭ - G♭	A♭ - C♭ - E♭♭ - G♭	A♭ - C♭ - E♭♭ - G♭♭
A	A - C# - E - G#	A - C# - E - G	A - C - E - G	A - C - E♭ - G	A - C - E♭ - G♭
B♭	B♭ - D - F - A	B♭ - D - F - A♭	B♭ - D♭ - F - A♭	B♭ - D♭ - F♭ - A♭	B♭ - D♭ - F♭ - A♭♭
B	B - D# - F# - A#	B - D# - F# - A	B - D - F# - A	B - D - F - A	B - D - F - A♭
C♭	C♭ - E♭ - G♭ - B♭	C♭ - E♭ - G♭ - B♭♭	C♭ - E♭♭ - G♭ - B♭♭	C♭ - E♭♭ - G♭♭ - B♭♭	C♭ - E♭♭ - G♭♭ - B♭♭♭

You can use the simpler keys to aid in memorizing the more complex ones. For instance, a C dominant 7th chord is C-E-G-B♭. If you lower the C to C♭, you need to lower all the other notes one half step as well. So, a C♭ dominant 7th chord would simply be a half step lower than C—so, the C♭ dominant 7th would be written as C♭-E♭-G♭-B♭♭.

As you can see from the chart, a C♭ diminished 7th chord is C♭-E♭♭-G♭♭-B♭♭♭! Let me be the first to say that anything that has to involve triple flats is ridiculous…write it in B! From here on, C♭ will be deleted…you know enough about it already! Hey, while we're at it, let's throw out D♭ and G♭…if you need them, just think in C# or F#, then transpose. Now's a good time to use those enharmonic equivalents!

DIMINISHED 7TH CHORD	ENHARMONIC EQUIVALENT
C♭ - E♭♭ - G♭♭ - B♭♭♭	B - D - F - A♭
C - E♭ - G♭ - B♭♭	B♯ - D♯ - F♯ - A
D♭ - F♭ - A♭♭ - C♭♭	C♯ - E - G - B♭
E♭ - G♭ - B♭♭ - D♭♭	D♯ - F♯ - A - C
F - A♭ - C♭ - E♭♭	E♯ - G♯ - B - D
G♭ - B♭♭ - D♭♭ - F♭♭	F♯ - A - C - E♭
A♭ - C♭ - E♭♭ - G♭♭	G♯ - B - D - F
B♭ - D♭ - F♭ - A♭♭	A♯ - C♯ - E - G

Even though the B♯, D♯, E♯, G♯ and A♯ major scales are not all that useful, it's good to be able to think in those keys as well, because when a flat key becomes overrun with flats, it's sometimes easier to think of the enharmonic equivalent.

HOW TO "HIP UP" 7TH CHORDS

If you've tried playing some of these chords on the piano, you may not be too impressed. The sound of the chords in **root position** (with the root [1] of the chord as the bottom note) is not all-that-great a sound. It's sort of like eating a handful of flour, and wondering why it doesn't taste like cake! Here's how to "spice up" the 7th chord:

1. **Get out of root position.**

A C major 7th chord in root position would be C-E-G-B. If you play the chord in **1st inversion** (with the 3rd as the bottom note), it would be E-G-B-C. This has a little more dissonance (because of the B and C being played next to each other), but in this case the dissonance is desirable, making the chord more interesting. **2nd inversion** would be G-B-C-E, and **3rd inversion** would be B-C-E-G. All of these inversions will sound better than the root position chord.

With each of these chords (played with your right hand), play the root an octave or two lower with your left hand. The left hand will be performing the role of a bass player in the band. It's important to note that the chords you play are **not** true inversions, since the bass note will remain the root. Rather, these inversions are variations in **chord voicings**.

2. **Get rid of the root...add the 9th.**

The bass player (or your left hand) will be playing the root of the chord. Because of this, the root **is not necessary in the chord**. So dump it...but just to make the chord a little more interesting, play the 9th in place of the root!

"Hold on a second!" you say. "This book hasn't said anything about 9ths!" Well, you're right, but you've already seen them...a 9th is another name for a 2nd! The reason why it wouldn't be called a 2nd is **to maintain the tertian structure of the chord**. In English, it means that chords are built in 3rds (1,3,5,7,9,11,13), and so now 2nds=9ths, 4ths=11ths, and 6ths=13ths. Nothin' to it! So in the example E-G-B-C, change it to E-G-B-**D**. Don't forget to play a C down low with the left hand.

3. **Get rid of the 5th...add the 13th.**

Because of the overtone series (which I have neither the time nor inclination to explain in this book), the 5th is a note that **is heard without being played**. The bottom line is that you don't need it in your chord. You can leave it out and everything will work fine. But why stop there? Substitute a 13th (6th) for it. So now E-G-B-D becomes E-**A**-B-D (with C in the bass). Congratulations...you're now cool!

THE EXCEPTION TO THE RULE: Ya' gotta play the 5th if it's been altered. In other words, if the chord contains a ♭5 or ♯5, Keep it!

Remember that with each step, your chord becomes a little thicker-sounding. At some point you may decide it's **too** dense. Just back up to where you liked it last and use that. You may want to experiment with the sound of the true chord inversions, where the bass note gets changed (like a C major triad with E in the bass). For now, though, work on finding interesting chord voicings, and then try to play chord progressions, such as can be found in fake books or published music. Keep in mind that the best way to go from one chord to another is through smooth **voice leading**, which simply means trying to change chords with as little right hand motion as possible.

CHAPTER 5

Scale choices for chords...
what to play and when to play it

Now that you understand how to build chords, all you have to do is go back and fill in the spaces *between* the chord tones to figure out what scales to use.

Here's how it works: suppose you want to jam with another musician or a band. Once you've figured out where to rehearse, when to turn on the fog machine and the flashpots, how much to bribe the disgruntled neighbor, and who's buying the Chinese food, you still need to figure out *what to play*. If someone knows a song on their instrument, and you want to play along, you need to figure out the chord sequence. Once that's been done, you need to use scales that will coincide with the chords being played. This isn't hard to do.

We'll begin with 7th chords, because they're easier to figure out. Why? Because you only have to figure out three other notes to play (remember, 7th chords are four-note chords!). If you start with triads, you have to figure out four other notes.

First, a quick review of Chapter 4:

7th CHORD	NOTES FROM MAJOR SCALE			
Major	1	3	5	7
Dominant	1	3	5	♭7
Minor	1	♭3	5	♭7
Half-Diminished	1	♭3	♭5	♭7
Diminished	1	♭3	♭5	♭♭7

So, if your guitarist/keyboardist/ukelele-playin' buddy plays a major 7th chord, a major scale will probably work great:

Major scale (Ionian mode): **1** 2 **3** 4 **5** 6 **7** 8

All of the notes in the major 7th **chord** are represented, and the other notes allow you to play more melodically, instead of being stuck playing 1-3-5-7 all night.

There is one potential trouble spot, and that's the 4th. Remember the distance between 3 and 4 in a major scale? Right, a half step. So the guitarist/ keyboardist/ukelele-playin' buddy is pounding on a 3rd, and if you try to play a 4th a half step above, you experience something known as **dissonance**. This can be cool, if you harness it correctly. Generally speaking, you want to try and **resolve the dissonance**. In this case, if you play a 4th in your solo and stay on the 4th, it will not be resolved. However, if you play the 4th and resolve it down into the 3rd, it'll make good sense, and you'll be applauded for your good taste…well, maybe not, but you *will* be dealing with the 4th in a musical manner.

Now, suppose your guitarist/keyboardist/…you know what I mean! Suppose he/she plays a **dominant 7th chord**. Well, if you fill in the blanks, here's what you get:

Dominant scale (Mixolydian mode): **1** 2 **3** 4 5 6 ♭**7** 8

This has the same problem, and the same solution, as the major scale—4 needs to resolve to 3, because of the half step clash. Other than that, the scale works great.

Now, how's about dat dere minor 7th chord? Try this one:

Minor (Dorian) scale: **1** 2 ♭**3** 4 5 6 ♭**7** 8

The name of this scale is the Dorian mode. A mode is really just another name for a scale. This is the primary scale choice for a minor 7th chord. Since there are no notes a half step above a chord tone, every note in this scale works great. Any note can be sustained above the chord, without fear of dissonance. Later on, you may *want* that dissonance, but for now, stick to this scale and you won't go wrong.

Next is the half-diminished chord. There's a special **this week only** on this scale:

Half-diminished (Locrian) scale: **1** ♭2 ♭**3** 4 ♭**5** ♭6 ♭**7** 8

The only trouble spot is between 1 and ♭2. You could just play 2 instead of ♭2, but then it wouldn't be the Locrian mode…it would be something else I haven't the time to get into just now. So leave the ♭2 for now, and **resolve** it into 1. Thank you.

And finally the diminished 7th chord scale of choice:

Diminished scale: **1** 2 ♭**3** 4 ♭**5** ♭6 ♭♭**7** 7 8

For a diminished 7th chord, a diminished scale works well. A diminished scale goes whole step-half step all the way up, so an extra note has to be inserted in order to make it symmetrical. There are two 7s, one of which has been double-flatted. This is dangerous, and should only be undertaken by professionals…just kidding!

So, here's yet another half-a-chapter summary:

7th CHORD	RECOMMENDED SCALE CHOICE	SCALE STRUCTURE								
Major	Major scale	1	2	3	4	5	6	7	8	
Minor	Dorian mode	1	2	♭3	4	5	6	♭7	8	
Dominant	Mixolydian mode	1	2	3	4	5	6	♭7	8	
Half-diminished	Locrian mode	1	♭2	♭3	4	♭5	♭6	♭7	8	
Diminished	Diminished scale	1	2	♭3	4	♭5	♭6	♭♭7	7	8

Now, here's how to deal with the triads:

For a major triad...try a major scale.

For a minor triad...use the Dorian mode.

For a diminished triad...how 'bout a diminished scale?

The augmented triad is rarely used, so a rarely used scale fits it well:

Whole tone scale: **1** 2 **3** #4 **#5** b7 8

The whole tone scale is called that because there is a whole step between each note in the scale. In order to do this, one of the letter names in a normal scale has to be left out. Notice that there is no 6 in this scale. Since the 5th has been raised, and the 7th lowered, there's no room for 6. There is, however, a lovely condo in Cocoa Beach, with 2 1/2 baths and a sunken living room, which can sleep 5!

So, after all that talk, here's the end result:

CHORD	RECOMMENDED SCALE CHOICE	SCALE STRUCTURE								
Maj. triad	Major scale (Ionian Mode)	1	2	3	4	5	6	7	8	
Major 7th	Major scale (Ionian Mode)	1	2	3	4	5	6	7	8	
Dominant 7th	Mixolydian mode	1	2	3	4	5	6	b7	8	
Min. triad	Dorian mode	1	2	b3	4	5	6	b7	8	
Minor 7th	Dorian mode	1	2	b3	4	5	6	b7	8	
Aug. triad	Whole tone	1	2	3	#4	#5	b7	8		
Half-dim.	Locrian mode	1	b2	b3	4	b5	b6	b7	8	
Dim. triad	Diminished scale	1	2	b3	4	b5	b6	bb7	7	8
Diminished 7th	Diminished scale	1	2	b3	4	b5	b6	bb7	7	8

There, that wasn't so bad, was it?

You can customize a scale for a particular purpose. For instance, suppose you saw a chord that said C7♯11…whadda ya' do? Don't panic! First, you know that C7 can be handled by Mixolydian. Next, you should know that ♯11 is a chordal way of expressing ♯4 so…just ♯ **the 4!** Here's how it looks:

C Mixolydian: C D E F G A B♭ C
becomes C D E **F♯** G A B♭ C!!!

*******BONUS ROUND*******

Included next are the formulas for five more scales!
   • Pentatonics (major and minor)
   • The Blues Scale
   • Minor Scales (Melodic and Harmonic)

Pentatonics and Blues Scale

"Penta" means five… "tonic" means tone. So, a pentatonic scale is a five-tone scale! To get a major pentatonic, simply take a **major** scale, and get rid of 4 and 7.

Major Scale:	1	2	3	4	5	6	7	8
Major Scale without 4 and 7:	1	2	3	-	5	6	-	8
Major Pentatonic:	1	2	3	5	6	8		

The minor pentatonic is a little more complex. To get a minor pentatonic, simply take a Dorian scale, and get rid of 2 and 6.

Minor Pentatonic: 1   ♭3   4   5   ♭7   8

The blues scale is just like the minor pentatonic, with one additional note.

Blues scale: 1   ♭3   4   ♯4   5   ♭7   8

Harmonic and Melodic Minor

These scales are used primarily in classical music. The modes of these scales, however, are extremely useful.

Harmonic minor: 1   2   ♭3   4   5   ♭6   7   8

The melodic minor is the only scale that is played differently coming down from how it's played going up!

Melodic minor (ascending):   1   2   ♭3   4   5   6   7   8
Melodic minor (descending):   8   ♭7   ♭6   5   4   ♭3   2   1

Descending melodic minor is also known as pure minor, or the Aeolian mode. Since the descending form is redundant (a mode of the major scale—see Chapter 7), jazz musicians concern themselves exclusively with the ascending form.

Let's see it again in slow motion:

SCALE	STRUCTURE	EXAMPLE IN C
Major Pentatonic	1 2 3 5 6 8	C D E G A C
Minor Pentatonic	1 ♭3 4 5 ♭7 8	C E♭ F G B♭ C
Blues Scale	1 ♭3 4 ♯4 5 ♭7 8	C E♭ F F♯ G B♭ C
Harmonic Minor	1 2 ♭3 4 5 ♭6 7 8	C D E♭ F G A♭ B C
Melodic Minor (Ascending)	1 2 ♭3 4 5 6 7 8	C D E♭ F G A B C
Melodic Minor (Descending)	8 ♭7 ♭6 5 4 ♭3 2 1	C B♭ A♭ G F E♭ D C

The pentatonics (and blues scale) are the primary scale choices of pop, r&b, and blues music. Once you start hearing what the scales sound like, you'll recognize them everywhere…Lynyrd Skynyrd, Wilson Pickett, B.B. King…they've all used them!

CHAPTER 6

Nomenclature...
the secret jazz decoder ring

You've got the idea for a song. You've worked out the chords you want to use on your zither. Now you want to teach the song to the rest of the band. So, you rent out a rehearsal hall at Gouge 'Em Studios and lug all your gear there. You spend half an hour getting the monitors right ("test…test…onetwoonetwo…it's still a little boomy!"), while the drummer gets his hair braided. At long last, it's time to teach your new song to the band!

"O.K.," you say, "I want a G major triad for the first two measures, followed by a bar of F major triad, and then a bar of C major triad. I want that whole progression played 8 times. Then, when we get to the bridge…"

"Wait a minute," says the guitar player. "What was that second chord?"

The bass player yells out, "Aw dude, let's just play Freebird!"

You get mad, because you're sick of playing Freebird, so as soon as the bass player steps into the puddle of water, you pull down the power switch on the breaker box, sending 220 volts coursing through his body and…

See, if you're not careful, making music can get real ugly. There's a better way, though. It's called music nomenclature.

Nomenclature (or **chord symbols**) is nothing more than a method of using symbols to indicate chord quality. Put even more simply, it's a way to speed up rehearsals and avoid frying your bass player.

Here's how it works. Each chord quality that has been covered in earlier chapters has an abbreviation or a symbol to represent it:

CHORD QUALITY	CHORD SYMBOL(S)	EXAMPLE IN C
Major	Nothing, tri	C, Ctri
Minor	min, m, -	Cmin, Cm, C-
Augmented	aug, +	Caug, C+
Diminished	dim, °	Cdim, C°
Major 7th	M7, Maj7, $\triangle$7	CM7, CMaj7, C$\triangle$7
Dominant	7	C7
Minor 7th	m7, min 7, -7	Cm7, Cmin7, C-7
Half-Diminished	min7♭5, ø	Cmin7♭5, C$^{\varnothing}$
Diminished 7th	dim7, °7	Cdim7, C°7

This is the secret code musicians have been using for years.

Now that you know the chords, it's time to implement them in a chart, or "road map", as it is sometimes referred to. At this point, it might be a good idea to get a little working knowledge on reading music. There are plenty of good books out there on the subject, and since the focus of this book is on theory and improvisation, reading music will be glossed over. However, there's no getting away from it completely:

Beat: A unit of time (that pounding noise your neighbor annoys you with when he listens to Depeche Mode!).

Measure (or **bar**): A group of beats (usually four). When the Beatles sang "one, two, three, four" before "I Saw Her Standing There," they were giving a one-measure introduction before the song, or a one-bar intro for short. In a waltz tempo, there are only three beats per measure (boom,click,click).

Bar Line: A vertical line [|] that separates the measures. Also, what happens when the band takes a break!

O.K., now it's time to go back to the original song you wrote on the zither (are you in the zither union?). You wanted a G major triad for 2 measures:

G
| / / / / | / / / / | ...And that's it! (Notice the hash marks [/] represent beats.)

Next, you want a measure of F major triad, and one of C:

G   F   C
| / / / / | / / / / | / / / / | / / / / |

Now you want them to repeat this progression. If you wanted it played twice, you'd just add a **repeat sign**:

```
G        F    C
I / / / / I / / / / I / / / / I / / / / :II
```

…Since you need it played a total of eight times, you just write that in above the repeat sign:

```
G          F    C    8x
I / / / / I / / / / I / / / / I / / / / :II  …and you're ready to rock 'n' roll!
```

Remember, for a major triad all you need is the key of the chord. However, if you want to ensure that they don't play a major 7th chord, you may want to be more specific:

```
Gtri         Ftri   Ctri   8x
I / / / / I / / / / I / / / / I / / / / :II
```

This is usually preferable if you're working with jazz musicians, since they like to "beef up" the sound of the chord as much as possible. In pop music circles, if you ask for an F chord, chances are good that you'll get an F major triad.

So, that's it. You can use this information to write chord progressions out for your musician friends, to jot down an idea before it disappears (that'll happen a lot!), and to "decode" music in fake books or chord charts. Enjoy!

CHAPTER 7

Modes of the major scale...
more bang for your buck

Suppose you loaned $12 to your best friend. When the time comes for him to give back the money, he gives you $84. When you ask if he's recently been near a nuclear power plant, he says, "Well, I made a couple of investments, and I managed to **septuple** your money!"

You've worked hard to soak up all the information so far. It's about time you caught a break! Here it is:

Let's take a C major scale (which, by the way, is also known as the **Ionian mode**). Now, instead of playing the scale from C to C, play it from D to D:

D E F G A B C D

The structure of a major scale is 1 2 3 4 5 6 7 8. The structure of this **new** scale (compared to D major) is 1 2 ♭3 4 5 6 ♭7 8.

Since the
notes are the same as those in the C major scale, this is called a **mode** of the C major scale. Specifically, this is the 2nd mode, known as the **Dorian mode**.

Next, play a C major scale starting on E:

E F G A B C D E

49

Compare this to the E major scale, and you'll see this mode is 1 ♭2 ♭3 4 5 ♭6 ♭7 8. The name of this, the 3rd mode, is the **Phrygian mode**.

Now, start a C major scale on F:

F G A B C D E F

This is an F major scale, with a ♯4. The 4th mode is called the **Lydian mode**.

The 5th mode looks like this:

G A B C D E F G

Again, very close to the parallel major, but this time it's a ♭7 that distinguishes it. This is the **Mixolydian mode**.

The 6th mode is:

A B C D E F G A

Comparing this to an A major scale, you get 1 2 ♭3 4 5 ♭6 ♭7 8. This is the Aeolian mode. This is also known as **pure** or **natural minor**.

Finally, the 7th mode of a C major scale is:

B C D E F G A B

This is quite a bit different than a B major scale. The structure is 1 ♭2 ♭3 4 ♭5 ♭6 ♭7 8. This is the **Locrian mode**.

In summary:

MODE NAME	STRUCTURE OF MODE							
IONIAN	1	2	3	4	5	6	7	8
DORIAN	1	2	♭3	4	5	6	♭7	8
PHRYGIAN	1	♭2	♭3	4	5	♭6	♭7	8
LYDIAN	1	2	3	♯4	5	6	7	8
MIXOLYDIAN	1	2	3	4	5	6	♭7	8
AEOLIAN	1	2	♭3	4	5	♭6	♭7	8
LOCRIAN	1	♭2	♭3	4	♭5	♭6	♭7	8

So, before you start cursing in Greek (they came up with the names), think about this–a simple C major scale delivers **7 modes**! If you were to go through this with each of the major scales (12, not counting enharmonics), you'd get this:

7 (modes) x 12 (keys) = **84 scales**!!!

After working hard to learn to play your major scales, you now have access to 7 times as many scales as you thought you did! All for no extra charge!!

Let's keep C as the starting note, and apply the formulas:

MODE NAME	STRUCTURE OF MODE								EXAMPLE IN C							
IONIAN	1	2	3	4	5	6	7	8	C	D	E	F	G	A	B	C
DORIAN	1	2	♭3	4	5	6	♭7	8	C	D	E♭	F	G	A	B♭	C
PHRYGIAN	1	♭2	♭3	4	5	♭6	♭7	8	C	D♭	E♭	F	G	A♭	B♭	C
LYDIAN	1	2	3	♯4	5	6	7	8	C	D	E	F♯	G	A	B	C
MIXOLYDIAN	1	2	3	4	5	6	♭7	8	C	D	E	F	G	A	B♭	C
AEOLIAN	1	2	♭3	4	5	♭6	♭7	8	C	D	E♭	F	G	A♭	B♭	C
LOCRIAN	1	♭2	♭3	4	♭5	♭6	♭7	8	C	D♭	E♭	F	G♭	A♭	B♭	C

For those of you who have read Chapter 5, you'll recognize several of these modes. Now, let's see what kinds of 7th chords are generated from each mode:

MODE NAME	STRUCTURE OF MODE								7TH CHORD IN C
IONIAN	1	2	3	4	5	6	7	8	C - E - G - B
DORIAN	1	2	♭3	4	5	6	♭7	8	C - E♭ - G - B♭
PHRYGIAN	1	♭2	♭3	4	5	♭6	♭7	8	C - E♭ - G - B♭
LYDIAN	1	2	3	♯4	5	6	7	8	C - E - G - B
MIXOLYDIAN	1	2	3	4	5	6	♭7	8	C - E - G - B♭
AEOLIAN	1	2	♭3	4	5	♭6	♭7	8	C - E♭ - G - B♭
LOCRIAN	1	♭2	♭3	4	♭5	♭6	♭7	8	C - E♭ - G♭ - B♭

By dividing the 7th chords into their respective families, you can see where the scales can be useful:

MAJOR 7TH
Ionian (major scale)
Lydian (major scale with $\sharp$4)

DOMINANT
Mixolydian (major scale with $\flat$7)

MINOR 7TH
Dorian ($\flat$3, $\flat$7)
Phrygian ($\flat$2, $\flat$3, $\flat$6, $\flat$7)
Aeolian ($\flat$3, $\flat$6, $\flat$7)

HALF-DIMINISHED
Locrian ($\flat$2, $\flat$3, $\flat$5, $\flat$6, $\flat$7)

So, the lowly major scale is capable of generating modes useful for four of the five 7th chords! Now, let's look closer at the three modes not covered in Chapter 5:

Lydian (1 2 3 $\sharp$4 5 6 7 8)

This scale is an extremely popular scale with jazz musicians. Remember that a major scale has one note that needs to be treated carefully (the 4th)? Well, the Lydian mode eliminates that by raising the 4th a half step.

Aeolian (1 2 $\flat$3 4 5 $\flat$6 $\flat$7 8)

Also known as pure minor, or natural minor (or the descending form of melodic minor, but that's another chapter!). This is not quite as useful as Dorian, but if you do use it, be careful with the $\flat$6, which is a half step above the 5th.

Phrygian (1 $\flat$2 $\flat$3 4 5 $\flat$6 $\flat$7 8)

Again, not as common as Dorian, but it's used a lot in ethnic music. It'll give you an East European kind of sound. The $\flat$2 needs to resolve into 1, and $\flat$6 into 5.

Wow! Betcha didn't think you could do all that, eh? $12 well spent!

CHAPTER 8

Intervals...musical geometry

When discussing the distance between two notes, it becomes tedious to say "four whole steps" or "the first and the sixth note of a major scale." That's where intervals come in.

In a major scale, there are three different types of intervals: major, minor and perfect. You may ask, why does there have to be an interval other than major or minor? What makes an interval 'perfect'? You are already saying, "Oh-oh, so far I can understand this theory stuff. Now comes the hard part."

All right, so it's a little complex…but not too bad. Let's look at a major scale:
1 2 3 4 5 6 7 8

If you were to play 1 while someone else played the same note, you would be playing a **perfect unison** (also called a **perfect prime**).

Now, the distance from 1 to 2 is a whole step. It's also known as a **major 2nd**.

From 1 to 3 is two whole steps, or 2 steps, for short. This is a **major 3rd**.

From 1 to 4 is 2 1/2 steps. This is a **perfect 4th**.

From 1 to 5 is 3 1/2 steps. This is a **perfect 5th**.

From 1 to 6 is 4 1/2 steps. This is a **major 6th**.

From 1 to 7 is 5 1/2 steps. This is a **major 7th**.

From 1 to 8 is 6 steps. This is a **perfect octave**.

Got all that? It's really not that hard.

INTERVAL	NUMBER OF STEPS	EXAMPLE FROM C
Major 2nd	1	C up to D
Major 3rd	2	C up to E
Perfect 4th	2 1/2	C up to F
Perfect 5th	3 1/2	C up to G
Major 6th	4 1/2	C up to A
Major 7th	5 1/2	C up to B

Now, the thing to notice is that intervals of unison (1), 4ths, 5ths, and octaves (8) can be perfect. Intervals of 2nds, 3rds, 6ths and 7ths can be major. However, you can't have a major 4th. You also couldn't have a perfect 2nd. Now, look what happens when these intervals are altered:

Take a major 2nd interval, C up to D. If you were to lower the D to D♭, you would have a **minor 2nd**. Also, if you kept the D, and raised the C to C♯, you would again have a **minor 2nd**. So, **any major interval that is decreased in size by a half step becomes minor.**

One thing to remember at this point is that the letter names are crucial in order for this to work. For instance, C♯ up to D is a minor 2nd, but D♭ up to D isn't. It would be an **augmented** unison, because the letter names are the same. This rule applies to all intervals.

Let's go back to the major 2nd interval, C up to D. If you raise the D to D♯, you would now have C up to D♯, an **augmented 2nd**. Also, if you kept the D, and lowered the C to C♭, you would again have an **augmented 2nd**. So, **any major interval that is increased in size by a half step becomes augmented.** Notice that it's C up to D♯, not E♭. C up to E♭ would be a **minor 3rd**, because the **letter names are a third apart.**

56

So, in conclusion, major intervals, when reduced by a half step, become minor. When major intervals are expanded by a half step, they become augmented.

PERFECTO!

Now, what about perfect intervals? Well, take C up to F, a perfect 4th. If you raise the F up to F#, you now have C up to F#, an **augmented 4th**. If you lower the F to F♭, you would have C up to F♭, a **diminished 4th**. So, perfect intervals, when expanded by a half step, become augmented. Also, when perfect intervals are reduced in size by a half step, they become diminished.

It's about time for another chart:

Decrease a half step   **Increase a half step**

Diminished -----------Perfect -----------Augmented

One more thing: **Minor intervals, when decreased by a half step, become diminished.** Also, **Major intervals, when increased by a half step, become augmented**. So let's see how that looks:

1/2   1/2   1/2

Diminished   Minor   Major   Augmented

The major scale contains all of the major, minor, and perfect intervals. Here's where they are:

INTERVAL   **LOCATION(S) IN MAJOR SCALE**

Minor 2nd

```
1   2   3   4   5   6   7   8
        └─┘               └─┘
```

Major 2nd

```
1   2   3   4   5   6   7   8
└───┴───┘       └───┴───┴───┘
```

Minor 3rd

```
1   2   3   4   5   6   7   1   2
    └───────┘       └───────┘
        └───────┘       └───────┘
```

Major 3rd

```
1   2   3   4   5   6   7   8
    └───────┘   └───────┘
        └───────┘
```

Perfect 4th

```
1   2   3   4   5   6   7   1   2   3
    └───────────┘   └───────────┘
        └───────────┘   └───────────┘
            └───────────┘   └───────────┘
```

Perfect 5th

```
                    ┌───────────────┐
1   2   3   4   5   6   7   1   2   3
    └───────────────┘   └───────────────┘
        └───────────────┘
            └───────────────┘
                └───────────────┘
```

Minor 6th

```
            ┌───────────────────┐
1   2   3   4   5   6   7   1   2   3   4   5
                └───────────────────┘
                    └───────────────────┘
```

But wait, there's more…

58

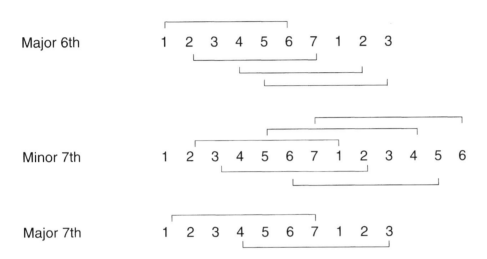

Major 6th   1 2 3 4 5 6 7 1 2 3

Minor 7th   1 2 3 4 5 6 7 1 2 3 4 5 6

Major 7th   1 2 3 4 5 6 7 1 2 3

It looks complex, but notice that the total location of any two major/minor intervals of the same distance (2nds, 3rds) will always total 7. For instance, there are three minor 6th possibilities, and four major 6th ones…yup, it equals 7 all right. That's because there are 7 notes in the scale.

The main thing to remember is that the size of the distance between two notes will always be determined by the letter names. B up to C will always be a 2nd…it doesn't matter if it's B♯ to C♯, or B♯ to C♭…it's still a 2nd!

Now, starting with C, look at all the major, minor and perfect intervals both **above and below:**

INTERVAL	ABOVE C	BELOW C
MINOR 2ND	D♭	B
MAJOR 2ND	D	B♭
MINOR 3RD	E♭	A
MAJOR 3RD	E	A♭
PERFECT 4TH	F	G
PERFECT 5TH	G	F
MINOR 6TH	A♭	E
MAJOR 6TH	A	E♭
MINOR 7TH	B♭	D
MAJOR 7TH	B	D♭

Notice how a strong knowledge of all the major scales can help speed up the process of looking for the answer. For instance, if you know that C is the 2nd note of a B♭ major

scale,then you know that C down to B♭ is a major 2nd. Try this chart on your own, with a different starting note. How quickly can you come up with the answers?

Still not sure about all this? Here's the same chart, only this time using E as the starting note (E is a great rock 'n' roll note!)

INTERVAL	ABOVE E	BELOW E
MINOR 2ND	F	D#
MAJOR 2ND	F#	D
MINOR 3RD	G	C#
MAJOR 3RD	G#	C
PERFECT 4TH	A	B
PERFECT 5TH	B	A
MINOR 6TH	C	G#
MAJOR 6TH	C#	G
MINOR 7TH	D	F#
MAJOR 7TH	D#	F

Pick 10 more starting notes, and you'll have 'em all. Just make sure you don't use an incorrect spelling. For instance, if you need the note a perfect 4th above F, it would be B♭, not A# (which would be an augmented third).

Now, take a look at chords.

Major chord: **1**(up a maj 3 to)**3**(up a min 3 to)**5**…**1**(up a perf 5 to)**5**…
…**3**(up a min 6 to)**8**

Minor chord: **1**(min 3)♭**3**(maj 3)**5**…**1**(perf 5)**5**…♭**3**(maj 6)**8**

61

Augmented chord: **1**(maj 3)**3**(maj 3)♯**5**...**1**(aug 5)♯**5**...**3**(min 6)**8**

Diminished chord: **1**(min 3)♭**3**(min 3)♭**5**...**1**(dim 5)♭**5**...♭**3**(maj 6)**8**

This is much easier to see on a music staff--assuming that you know how to **read** a music staff. If you don't, be sure to get my next book, "Son of Jazz Essentials--The Sequel---More Nuts, More Bolts, and Maybe Even A Torque Wrench!" Anyhow, this is what it looks like:

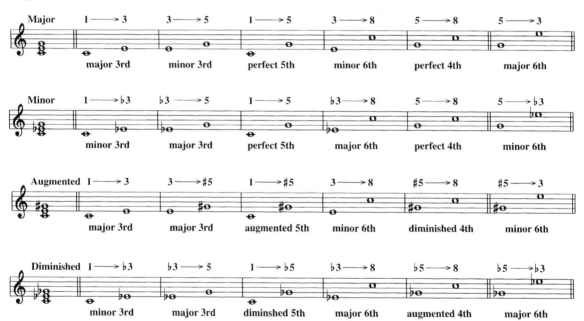

Now you can see where the names of the chords came from! Spend some time looking through the previous chapters, and see if you can identify intervals!

62

There's one very special interval that is the "halfway point" in an octave. Remember that the number of steps to an octave is six, right? Cut that in half, and three steps above a note will give you an **augmented 4th** or a **diminished 5th**. This is commonly called a "**tri-tone**" since its structure is three whole steps.

An augmented 4th above C is F♯, and a diminished 5th above C is G♭. F♯ and G♭ are **enharmonically equivalent** (remember that from Chapter 1?), which means that they sound the same, even though they're spelled differently. So, keeping all that in mind, take another look at a **dominant 7th chord**:

1(maj 3)**3**(min 3)**5**(min 3)♭**7**…**1**(perf 5)**5**…**3**(min 6)**8**…**5**(perf 4)**8**…**3**(TRI-TONE)♭**7**!!!

The tri-tone in a dominant chord is the engine that powers the chord!

The sound of 3 and ♭7 is fairly dissonant, but it's that tension that creates the great bluesy sound of the dominant chord. In fact, that's all you need (with the bass player/left hand playing the root (1) of the chord) to get the **sound** of the dominant chord.

Drill yourself, and work on speeding up the thought process. Ask questions like, "What's a perfect 4th above B♭?" and try to get to the point where you're able to get the answers instantly.

CHAPTER 8

Recommended materials... how to spend more money

If you're skimming through the book, and you've skipped straight to this chapter, you should be ashamed of yourself! Get back to work!!

If, on the other hand, you've busted your tail to learn the information in the previous chapters...you're probably due some Excedrin!

Let's see how you've done so far:

1. **Memorize the names of all the notes on the piano** (Chapter 1).

2. **Learn to spell major scales in all fifteen keys** (Chapter 2).

3. **Learn to spell triads in all keys** (Chapter 3).

4. **Learn to spell 7th chords in all keys** (Chapter 4).

5. **Learn the names and structures of the big five scales** (Chapter 5).

6. **Learn how to read (and write) chord changes and figure out what to do with them** (Chapters 5 and 6).

7. **Learn the secret superpowers of the major scale** (Chapter 7).

8. **Identify intervals, and know the distinction between enharmonic equivalents** (Chapter 8).

Excellent work! Now it's time for the fun stuff...

The basic concepts of improvisation:

Put simply, what you want to do when you improvise is "make the changes." When a series of chords is being played, you need to play the scale that corresponds to the chord being played **at the same time**. It's challenging, because there's a lot to think about...reading the chord, converting it in your mind to the scale of choice, remembering the structure of that particular scale, keeping track of how long to play before the next chord comes up...and, oh yeah, playing something interesting and musical at the same time!

The best way to get used to improvising is to limit the choices you have to make, so you can concentrate on one or two things at a time. Jamey Aebersold has a series of play-along CDs, with piano, bass, and drums providing background for **you** to improvise along with. Since you now know all of the major scales, start with Vol. 24 ("Major & Minor"). This is a set of two CDs, with the band playing in **one key** for 3-5 minutes. This means thinking only of C major, for instance.

Once you can play a scale, work on finding patterns within that scale. A great way to really learn a scale is to follow a twelve-step method from Aebersold's Vol. 1 "A New Approach to Jazz Improvisation," which I call:

"THE DIRTY DOZEN"

1. Play root/tonic note (1) of each scale .

2. Play first two notes of each scale.

3. Play first three notes of each scale.

4. Play first five notes of each scale.

5. Play triad of the scale (1,3, and 5 of the scale).

6. Play 7th chords (1,3,5, and 7th tones of the scale).

7. Play 9th chords (1,3,5,7, and 9th tones of the scale).

8. Play the entire scale up and down.

9. Play 6th chords (1,3,5, and 6th tones of the scale).

10. Play up the scale to the 9th and back down the chord tones.

11. Play up the 9th chord and then come back down the scale.

12. Play the scale in broken thirds (1,3…2,4…etc.) up and down.

You can put on a track of Vol. 24 and go through all twelve of these exercises, and you'll be in better control of the scale you're working on. After that, just play what you feel, keeping within the constraints of the scale, for starters. See what it feels like to make music instantly!

Find out what's hip in the jazz bin of your CD store:

Listening to jazz is the single most important thing you can do to learn the art of improvisation. Hundreds of jazz musicians have found their own way to express themselves through music. That expression can be analyzed, transcribed (written down), and learned through repetitive listening. As you get more accomplished on your instrument, you'll find that the amount of time it takes to understand what another player is doing will be less as you develop your ear.

It's not easy to generalize about who to listen to or what recordings to check out. One record label that has consistently put out quality product is Blue Note. If you find a recording on that label, chances are very good that you won't be disappointed. In addition, I've included my personal "desert island" collection:

1. **Saxophone Colossus**–Sonny Rollins

   I was at North Texas State when I first heard this album. My guitar playin' friend, Scott Sokoloff, loaned it to me. It took him six months to get it back. Sonny Rollins has a huge sound, and on this recording he is in total control. The rhythm section is superb, and the recording quality is excellent. Don't miss it!

2. **The Golden Years**–The Crusaders

   Wilton Felder's tenor sax is smooth, full bodied, and funky, in the "Texas Tenor" tradition. The music is an offshoot of the "Gospel Jazz" made popular by Horace Silver and Cannonball Adderley (two other monsters, by the way!). The Crusaders (originally The Jazz Crusaders) got a little too "discofied" in the late 70s-early 80s, but the bulk of their work is heartfelt and groove oriented. If you want to learn how to play blues/rock tenor sax, this is the textbook!

3. **Three Quartets**–Chick Corea

   This album will need a few listens to soak up everything, but it's well worth it. In addition to Corea on piano, the group consists of Steve Gadd on drums, Eddie Gomez on bass, and Michael Brecker on tenor sax. In addition to the Corea composition, it now includes a Brecker/Gadd version of Charlie Parker's **Confirmation**. The ensemble work is just awesome, and the solos are world-class.

4. **Kind of Blue**–Miles Davis

   This album has been hailed by many, and with good reason. The songs are simple in form, giving the soloists lots of room to create. For a lesson in how to utilize the Dorian mode, check out the song "So What". In addition to Miles on trumpet, you'll hear Bill Evans on piano, Cannonball Adderley on alto sax, and a little-known tenor saxophonist…John Coltrane!

5. **The Complete Concert '64**–Miles Davis

This is actually two albums in one. It was originally released as **My Funny Valentine** (which had all the slow songs from the concert) and **Four & More** (with all the up-tempo tunes). There was a lot of backstage feuding before this concert (detailed in the liner notes), which probably resulted in the high energy level on stage. Miles is at the top of his game, as are George Coleman (tenor sax), Herbie Hancock (piano), Ron Carter (bass), and Tony Williams (drums). You can hear the interplay between the band and the audience, with people shouting encouragement, much like a revival meeting. This was one of Miles's favorite recordings, too.

6. **Jaco Pastorius**–Jaco Pastorius

A man who completely redefined the electric bass, Jaco's presence can be heard in the playing of dozens of contemporary electric bassists. Jaco honed his style in Wayne Cochran's R&B band, which gave his jazz playing an interesting earthiness. As a result of this album, Jaco was invited to join the fusion jazz group **Weather Report**, founded by Wayne Shorter (sax) and Josef Zawinul (keyboards). The resulting group became the pinnacle of both Jaco and Weather Report's success, both musically and commercially.

7. **The History of**…–Art Blakey & The Jazz Messengers

Art Blakey's band was the "graduate school" of jazz musicians. Anyone who made it into the band was an exceptional talent, and when they left, they usually became band leaders themselves (some went on to get their "Doctorate" with Miles). There are so many great players in this collection. Check out Kenny Dorham, Clifford Brown, Lee Morgan, Bill Hardman, Freddie Hubbard, Woody Shaw, Valery Ponomarev, Wynton Marsalis…and those are just the trumpet players! A great place to start a CD collection.

8. **Speak No Evil**–Wayne Shorter

Freddie Hubbard (trumpet), Herbie Hancock (piano), Ron Carter (bass), Elvin Jones (drums), and Wayne Shorter (tenor sax). Recorded for Blue Note. That just about says it!

9. **Maiden Voyage**–Herbie Hancock

   I've always been a huge fan of Herbie's, so it comes as no surprise that he made it to four of my 10 "desert islands" **(Miles '64, Jaco, Speak No Evil)**. This is yet another premier Blue Note release, and many of Herbie's tunes are jazz war-horses, played at jazz clubs and wedding receptions alike.

10. **Lush Life**–Joe Henderson

    For those who say "what about something from *this* century." This was released in 1992, and it deservedly won a Grammy award for Joe (tenor sax), Wynton Marsalis (trumpet), Christian McBride (bass), Stephen Scott (piano), and Gregory Hutchinson (drums). This album gives you a glimpse into the future of contemporary jazz, and it looks great!

Wow, that was tough! I've got a stack of CDs I had to leave off, and they're so important that...well, here are the Honorable Mentions:

John Coltrane – **Blue Train**
Michael Brecker – **Michael Brecker**
Sonny Stitt - **Sits in with the Oscar Peterson Trio**
Charlie Parker – **Complete Savoy Recordings**
Cannonball Adderley – **Somethin' Else**
Weather Report – **Black Market**
Yellowjackets – **Yellowjackets**
Dexter Gordon – **The Homecoming**
Sonny Rollins – **A Night at the Village Vanguard**
Cannonball & Coltrane – **Limehouse Blues**

Now, the albums that my friends Mark Holter, Warren Sneed, Noe Marmolejo, Joel Fulgham, Todd Harrison, Claudia Burson, Dave Foster, and Kerry Movassagh recommend:

MARK'S LIST

Richie Cole – **Keeper of the Flame** or **Hollywood Madness**

Phil Woods – **Live at the Showboat**

Sonny Stitt, Sonny Rollins, Dizzy Gillespie – **Sonny Side Up**

Miles Davis – **Relaxin'** or **Cookin'** or **Steamin'**

Cannonball Adderley – **Bossa Rio Sextet**

Gene Ammons & Sonny Stitt – **Jug & Sonny**

Cannonball with Bill Evans – **Know What I Mean**

John Coltrane – **Ballads**

Pete Christlieb with Warne Marsh – **Apogee**

Jerry Bergonzi – **Standard Gonz**

WARREN'S LIST

John Coltrane – **Giant Steps**

Dexter Gordon – **A Swingin' Affair**

McCoy Tyner – **The Real McCoy** (with Joe Henderson)

Sonny Stitt – **The Champ**

John Coltrane – **Crescent**

The Quintet – **Jazz at Massey Hall** (Charlie Parker, Dizzy Gillespie, Bud Powell, Max Roach, Charlie Mingus)

Charlie Parker – **Bird (The original recordings of Charlie Parker)**

Joe Henderson – **The Kicker**

Mel Lewis – **& Friends**

Keith Jarrett – **Standards Vol. 1 & 2**

NOE'S LIST

Kenny Dorham – **Una Mas**

Joe Henderson – **In Japan**

Miles Davis – **Circle in the Round**

Joe Henderson – **Inner Urge**

Herbie Hancock – **Empyrean Isles**

Joe Henderson – **In 'n Out**

Chet Baker – **The Improviser**

Joe Henderson – **Page One**

Wayne Shorter – **Ju Ju**

Woody Shaw – **Lotus Flower**

JOEL'S LIST

Max Roach/Clifford Brown – **Daahoud**

Oliver Nelson – **Blues and the Abstract Truth** or **Big Band Live in Los Angeles**

Buddy Rich – **In London**

Thad Jones/Mel Lewis – **Suite for Pops**

Art Blakey – **Drum Suite**

The Hi Lo's – **& All That Jazz**

Chick Corea – **Friends** or **The Leprechaun**

Louie Bellson – **Big Band Explosion**

McCoy Tyner – **Supertrios**

Woody Shaw – **Rosewood**

Larry Young – **Zoltan**

TODD'S LIST

Thad Jones/Mel Lewis – **Live at Village Vanguard**

Miles Davis – **Bags' Groove** or **Round About Midnight**

John Coltrane – **Impressions**

Miles Davis – **Nefertiti**

Stan Getz – **Serenity** or **Anniversary**

J.J. Johnson – **Quintergy-Live at the Village Vanguard**

Buddy Rich – **Class of '77**

Wynton Marsalis – **Standards Vol. 1**

Tony Bennett – any release, especially **Bill Evans & Tony Bennett**

Steve Kuhn Trio – **Looking Back** (with Louis Nash)

CLAUDIA'S LIST

John Coltrane – **Lush Life** or **A Love Supreme** or **Johnny Hartman & John Coltrane**

Oscar Peterson – **Ella (Fitzgerald) & Oscar**

Sarah Vaughan – **A Brazilian Romance**

Bill Evans Trio – **At the Village Vanguard**

Thelonious Monk – **The London Collection**

Billy Holiday – **Lady Sings the Blues**

McCoy Tyner – **Song for My Lady**

Fathers & Sons – (a group session with the Marsalis brothers & dad…et. al.)

Charles Mingus – **Live at the Jazz Workshop**

George Benson – **Cookbook**

DAVE'S LIST

John Coltrane –**Transition** or **Live at the Village Vanguard**
Weather Report – **Night Passage**
Jimi Hendrix – **Are You Experienced**
Oscar Peterson – **Night Train**
Miles Davis – **We Want Miles**
Chick Corea – **Now He Sings, Now He Sobs**
Mike Stern – **Time in Place**
Eddie Daniels – **To Bird with Love**
John Scofield – **What We Do**
Marc Johnson – **Bass Desires**

KERRY'S LIST

Horace Silver – **Song for My Father**
Keith Jarrett – **Standards Live**
Pat Metheny/Dave Holland/Roy Haynes – **Question & Answer**
Wes Montgomery – **The Incredible Jazz Guitar Of**
Robben Ford – **Talk to Your Daughter**
Ornette Coleman – **Song X**
John Scofield – **Roughhouse** or **Bartok**
John Zorn – **Naked City**
Larry Carlton – **Strikes Twice**
Arthur Blythe – **Hipmotism**

Note: Most of these titles are available on CD.

What to do when you've finished this book:
Well, you should definitely collect as many Aebersold play-alongs as you can afford, and try to play with other instrumentalists to start developing your musical communication skills.

There are any number of excellent books for more in-depth jazz theory. Ask your friends what book they recommend. Even better, ask your music teacher in your school. You can always check out your local library to see what they have. Going to your local music store is not a bad idea, either. The point is, you are right at the beginning of a very enlightening journey. Keep the momentum going.

It's hard to get enough time on your instrument, so if you can get a good solid fifteen to twenty minutes a day, that's better than a sloppy hour a day. Practice over the full range of your instrument, and in all keys. Here's a way to get all the major scales over with quickly!:

ALL MAJOR SCALES IN UNDER 5 MINUTES
C major scale (up and down), C♯/D♭ scale (up and down), D major (up and down), etc., through all keys. When you're coming down, the last note should be the first of the new key. So, C coming down would be C B A G F E D **C♯ D♯ etc...**

If you go to a traditional college and major in music, you'll take music theory, and more than likely an ear training class. To prepare for that, go back to the triads and work on identifying between the four types by ear. It's not hard, especially if you practice them on your instrument. Try this pattern:

TRIAD EXERCISE/HORN-FINGERS WARM-UP
Major(up and down), minor(up and down), augmented(up and down), diminished(up and down). Repeat this procedure up a half step; continue through all keys.

Example in C:
C-E-G-E-C, C-E♭-G-E♭-C, C-E-G♯-E-C, C-E♭-G♭-E♭-C. (UP A HALF STEP)–C♯-E♯-G♯, **etc.**

Go through that, and in addition to cussing me out, you will begin to really hear the differences between the triads. Once you feel comfortable with this, you could go through and do the same thing with 7th chords. You could do the scale exercise, substituting one of the modes for the major scale, and get comfortable with the sound and the feel of the new scale. There are dozens of ideas for patterns that you can get from these exercises, and you'll have a better physical command of your instrument when you can play these effortlessly.

In order to strengthen your "inner clock", it's crucial that you **PRACTICE WITH A METRONOME OR DRUM MACHINE!!!!** The pulse of music is **so** important…if you plan on playing with other musicians, there has to be a common sense of time in order for everything to sync together. While none of us is perfect, the drum machine or metronome **will** be perfect (some would say **too** perfect!). Consistent use of these "machines" will help you recognize when the pulse of the music is slowing down or speeding up, and if you play with quality musicians, the minor adjustments will be seamless. If you have a good "time-feel" or "groove", the other players will be able to "lock in" with what you're playing. So make the drummer's job easier, and do your practicing with a consistent time source.

It's a good idea to get together with a private instructor who can help you through some of the pitfalls of an instrument. It's always good to have someone from the outside help with problem solving, especially when that person has been down the same road. Remember, no one sounds great the first time they play an instrument (well, maybe Mozart did), so don't be discouraged when you sound like a farm animal. We all did at some point! Enjoy the challenge, and you'll get it!!

Learn the name of a really good pizza place in Moline, IL:
Well, this is actually a trick question, because if you want **really** good pizza, you've gotta travel a bit. The latest addition in the "great pizza" category is **Uncle Bill's** in Geneseo and Davenport. Mention my name and get extra parmesan! For the all-time classics, go to Rock Island (**Harris [#1]**) or Sylvis (**Frank's**).   My wife insists on including **Happy Joe's** in Moline for their Taco Pizza, but I'm of the opinion that "Taco" and "Pizza" shouldn't be on the same menu! If you're from Moline and you disagree with me…too bad! Write your own book!

Well, it's been fun. I hope you've gotten all of this information. Repetition is the key to a lot of this, so try and get through the "boring" stuff, because the interesting stuff can't be realized without it. Good luck!

CHAPTER 10

Study sheets...gentlemen, start your triads

Wait, don't use this chapter!!! Go to your friendly neighborhood copy shop and make many copies, so you can reuse the worksheets. Or better still, have these pages laminated, and you can save a tree or two!!

The following is a means of testing to make sure you've soaked up all the pertinent information presented prior to this page (say that ten times fast!).

The first item will be a one-page overview of all the music theory covered in Chapters 3-5. You could've ripped out this page and not paid for the book, but that wouldn't have been nice, and besides, you would've missed all those great jokes included…hmm, better not push that angle. Anyhow, the **CHORDS AND CHORD/SCALE RELATIONSHIPS** chart is a great way to see the whole tamale (vegetarian, of course) in one shot.

Next, the fun begins. How much have you really learned so far? The litmus test is how quickly you can write down the information. The first worksheet covers enharmonic equivalents and major scales. These need to be worked on first, because everything else hinges on your knowledge of these. When you've become proficient at these (when you got 'em licked), go for the triads, and then 7th chords. Next are Mixolydian and Dorian modes, and finally Locrian and diminished scales (you can use these same worksheets to work on the scales covered in Chapter 7, too). When you're able to make par every time, you're finished with this book and ready for the next level, covered in Chapter 9. Thanks are not necessary (tips are!). Places, everybody!

PAR FOR THE COURSE	
Worksheet	**Par (minutes!)**
Enharmonics/Major Scales	3:00
Triads	5:00
7th Chords	9:00
Mixolydian/Dorian	5:00
Locrian/Diminished	9:00

CHORDS AND CHORD/SCALE RELATIONSHIPS
TRIADS

CHORD SYMBOL	TYPE OF CHORD	NUMBERS FROM MAJOR SCALE			EXAMPLE IN C		
C,C△,C MAJ	Major	1	3	5	C	E	G
C-,C min	Minor	1	♭3	5	C	E♭	G
C+,C aug	Augmented	1	3	♯5	C	E	G♯
C°, C dim	Diminished	1	♭3	♭5	C	E♭	G♭

7TH CHORDS (triads with added 7ths)

CHORD SYMBOL	TYPE OF CHORD	NUMBERS FROM MAJOR SCALE				EXAMPLE IN C			
C,C△,C Maj 7	Major 7th	1	3	5	7	C	E	G	B
C7	Dominant 7th	1	3	5	♭7	C	E	G	B♭
C-7,C min 7	Minor 7th	1	♭3	5	♭7	C	E♭	G	B♭
Cø, C min 7 ♭5	Half-Diminished	1	♭3	♭5	♭7	C	E♭	G♭	B♭
C°7, C dim 7	Diminished	1	♭3	♭5	♭♭7	C	E♭	G♭	B♭♭

BASIC SCALE CHOICES	ALTERATIONS TO MAJOR SCALE	EXAMPLE IN C
Major—Ionian (Major Scale)	1 2 3 4 5 6 7 8	C D E F G A B C
Dominant—Mixolydian	1 2 3 4 5 6 ♭7 8	C D E F G A B♭ C
Minor—Dorian	1 2 ♭3 4 5 6 ♭7 8	C D E♭ F G A B♭ C
Half-Diminished—Locrian	1 ♭2 ♭3 4 ♭5 ♭6 ♭7 8	C D♭ E♭ F G♭ A♭ B♭ C
Dim—Diminished Scale*	1 2 ♭3 4 ♭5 ♭6 ♭♭7 7 8	C D E♭ F G♭ A♭ B♭♭ B C
Aug—Whole Tone Scale**	1 2 3 ♯4 ♯5 ♭7 8	C D E F♯ G♯ B♭ C

*The dim. scale is a symmetrical scale, alternating whole step-half step, or half step-whole step.

**The whole tone scale is also symmetrical, with whole steps all the way up!

Spell enharmonic equivalents:

B♭=	G♯=	C♯=	D♯=	F♯=	E♭=	A♭=
B♯=	G♭=	A♯=	D♭=	F♭=	C♭=	E♯=

Spell Major Scales (Ionian Modes):

C   _____ _____ _____ _____ _____ _____   C

C♯   _____ _____ _____ _____ _____ _____   C♯

D♭   _____ _____ _____ _____ _____ _____   D♭

D   _____ _____ _____ _____ _____ _____   D

E♭   _____ _____ _____ _____ _____ _____   E♭

E   _____ _____ _____ _____ _____ _____   E

F   _____ _____ _____ _____ _____ _____   F

F♯   _____ _____ _____ _____ _____ _____   F♯

G♭   _____ _____ _____ _____ _____ _____   G♭

G   _____ _____ _____ _____ _____ _____   G

A♭   _____ _____ _____ _____ _____ _____   A♭

A   _____ _____ _____ _____ _____ _____   A

B♭   _____ _____ _____ _____ _____ _____   B♭

B   _____ _____ _____ _____ _____ _____   B

C♭   _____ _____ _____ _____ _____ _____   C♭

TRIADS

	MAJOR	MINOR	AUGMENTED	DIMINISHED
1. C	— — —	— — —	— — —	— — —
2. C#	— — —	— — —	— — —	— — —
3. Db	— — —	— — —	— — —	— — —
4. D	— — —	— — —	— — —	— — —
5. Eb	— — —	— — —	— — —	— — —
6. E	— — —	— — —	— — —	— — —
7. F	— — —	— — —	— — —	— — —
8. F#	— — —	— — —	— — —	— — —
9. Gb	— — —	— — —	— — —	— — —
10. G	— — —	— — —	— — —	— — —
11. Ab	— — —	— — —	— — —	— — —
12. A	— — —	— — —	— — —	— — —
13. Bb	— — —	— — —	— — —	— — —
14. B	— — —	— — —	— — —	— — —
15. Cb	— — —	— — —	— — —	— — —

7TH CHORDS

	MAJOR	DOMINANT	MINOR	1/2-DIMINISHED	DIMINISHED
1. C	_ _ _ _ _	_ _ _ _ _	_ _ _ _ _	_ _ _ _	_ _ _ _
2. C♯	_ _ _ _ _	_ _ _ _ _	_ _ _ _ _	_ _ _ _	_ _ _ _
3. D♭	_ _ _ _ _	_ _ _ _ _	_ _ _ _ _	_ _ _ _	_ _ _ _
4. D	_ _ _ _ _	_ _ _ _ _	_ _ _ _ _	_ _ _ _	_ _ _ _
5. E♭	_ _ _ _ _	_ _ _ _ _	_ _ _ _ _	_ _ _ _	_ _ _ _
6. E	_ _ _ _ _	_ _ _ _ _	_ _ _ _ _	_ _ _ _	_ _ _ _
7. F	_ _ _ _ _	_ _ _ _ _	_ _ _ _ _	_ _ _ _	_ _ _ _
8. F♯	_ _ _ _ _	_ _ _ _ _	_ _ _ _ _	_ _ _ _	_ _ _ _
9. G♭	_ _ _ _ _	_ _ _ _ _	_ _ _ _ _	_ _ _ _	_ _ _ _
10. G	_ _ _ _ _	_ _ _ _ _	_ _ _ _ _	_ _ _ _	_ _ _ _
11. A♭	_ _ _ _ _	_ _ _ _ _	_ _ _ _ _	_ _ _ _	_ _ _ _
12. A	_ _ _ _ _	_ _ _ _ _	_ _ _ _ _	_ _ _ _	_ _ _ _
13. B♭	_ _ _ _ _	_ _ _ _ _	_ _ _ _ _	_ _ _ _	_ _ _ _
14. B	_ _ _ _ _	_ _ _ _ _	_ _ _ _ _	_ _ _ _	_ _ _ _
15. C♭	_ _ _ _ _	_ _ _ _ _	_ _ _ _ _	_ _ _ _	_ _ _ _

Spell Mixolydian Modes:

C _____ _____ _____ _____ _____ _____ _____ C

C♯ _____ _____ _____ _____ _____ _____ _____ C♯

D♭ _____ _____ _____ _____ _____ _____ _____ D♭

D _____ _____ _____ _____ _____ _____ _____ D

E♭ _____ _____ _____ _____ _____ _____ _____ E♭

E _____ _____ _____ _____ _____ _____ _____ E

F _____ _____ _____ _____ _____ _____ _____ F

F♯ _____ _____ _____ _____ _____ _____ _____ F♯

G♭ _____ _____ _____ _____ _____ _____ _____ G♭

G _____ _____ _____ _____ _____ _____ _____ G

A♭ _____ _____ _____ _____ _____ _____ _____ A♭

A _____ _____ _____ _____ _____ _____ _____ A

B♭ _____ _____ _____ _____ _____ _____ _____ B♭

B _____ _____ _____ _____ _____ _____ _____ B

C♭ _____ _____ _____ _____ _____ _____ _____ C♭

Spell Dorian Modes:

C _____ _____ _____ _____ _____ _____ _____ C

C♯ _____ _____ _____ _____ _____ _____ _____ C♯

D♭ _____ _____ _____ _____ _____ _____ _____ D♭

D _____ _____ _____ _____ _____ _____ _____ D

E♭ _____ _____ _____ _____ _____ _____ _____ E♭

E _____ _____ _____ _____ _____ _____ _____ E

F _____ _____ _____ _____ _____ _____ _____ F

F♯ _____ _____ _____ _____ _____ _____ _____ F♯

G♭ _____ _____ _____ _____ _____ _____ _____ G♭

G _____ _____ _____ _____ _____ _____ _____ G

A♭ _____ _____ _____ _____ _____ _____ _____ A♭

A _____ _____ _____ _____ _____ _____ _____ A

B♭ _____ _____ _____ _____ _____ _____ _____ B♭

B _____ _____ _____ _____ _____ _____ _____ B

C♭ _____ _____ _____ _____ _____ _____ _____ C♭

After Mixolydian and Dorian, substitute any two of the following:
Phrygian, Lydian, Aeolian, Harmonic Minor, Melodic Minor (ascending).

Spell Locrian Modes: Spell Diminished Scales:

C   ___ ___ ___ ___ ___ ___ ___ C   C   ___ ___ ___ ___ ___ ___ ___ ___ C

C#   ___ ___ ___ ___ ___ ___ ___ C#   C#   ___ ___ ___ ___ ___ ___ ___ ___ C#

Db   ___ ___ ___ ___ ___ ___ ___ Db   Db   ___ ___ ___ ___ ___ ___ ___ ___ Db

D   ___ ___ ___ ___ ___ ___ ___ D   D   ___ ___ ___ ___ ___ ___ ___ ___ D

Eb   ___ ___ ___ ___ ___ ___ ___ Eb   Eb   ___ ___ ___ ___ ___ ___ ___ ___ Eb

E   ___ ___ ___ ___ ___ ___ ___ E   E   ___ ___ ___ ___ ___ ___ ___ ___ E

F   ___ ___ ___ ___ ___ ___ ___ F   F   ___ ___ ___ ___ ___ ___ ___ ___ F

F#   ___ ___ ___ ___ ___ ___ ___ F#   F#   ___ ___ ___ ___ ___ ___ ___ ___ F#

Gb   ___ ___ ___ ___ ___ ___ ___ Gb   Gb   ___ ___ ___ ___ ___ ___ ___ ___ Gb

G   ___ ___ ___ ___ ___ ___ ___ G   G   ___ ___ ___ ___ ___ ___ ___ ___ G

Ab   ___ ___ ___ ___ ___ ___ ___ Ab   Ab   ___ ___ ___ ___ ___ ___ ___ ___ Ab

A   ___ ___ ___ ___ ___ ___ ___ A   A   ___ ___ ___ ___ ___ ___ ___ ___ A

Bb   ___ ___ ___ ___ ___ ___ ___ Bb   Bb   ___ ___ ___ ___ ___ ___ ___ ___ Bb

B   ___ ___ ___ ___ ___ ___ ___ B   B   ___ ___ ___ ___ ___ ___ ___ ___ B

Cb   ___ ___ ___ ___ ___ ___ ___ Cb   Cb   ___ ___ ___ ___ ___ ___ ___ ___ Cb

Spell Major Pentatonic:

C	_____ _____ _____ _____	C
C#	_____ _____ _____ _____	C#
Db	_____ _____ _____ _____	Db
D	_____ _____ _____ _____	D
Eb	_____ _____ _____ _____	Eb
E	_____ _____ _____ _____	E
F	_____ _____ _____ _____	F
F#	_____ _____ _____ _____	F#
Gb	_____ _____ _____ _____	Gb
G	_____ _____ _____ _____	G
Ab	_____ _____ _____ _____	Ab
A	_____ _____ _____ _____	A
Bb	_____ _____ _____ _____	Bb
B	_____ _____ _____ _____	B
Cb	_____ _____ _____ _____	Cb

Spell Whole Tone:

C	_____ _____ _____ _____ _____	C
C#	_____ _____ _____ _____ _____	C#
Db	_____ _____ _____ _____ _____	Db
D	_____ _____ _____ _____ _____	D
Eb	_____ _____ _____ _____ _____	Eb
E	_____ _____ _____ _____ _____	E
F	_____ _____ _____ _____ _____	F
F#	_____ _____ _____ _____ _____	F#
Gb	_____ _____ _____ _____ _____	Gb
G	_____ _____ _____ _____ _____	G
Ab	_____ _____ _____ _____ _____	Ab
A	_____ _____ _____ _____ _____	A
Bb	_____ _____ _____ _____ _____	Bb
B	_____ _____ _____ _____ _____	B
Cb	_____ _____ _____ _____ _____	Cb

After Major Pentatonic, try Minor Pentatonic.

Answer keys (hey, no fair lookin' here first…go try on your own!!
Ionian (major scales)
Formula: 1 2 3 4 5 6 7 8
Answers: See page 21

Dorian
Formula: 1 2 ♭3 4 5 6 ♭7 8

C	D	E♭	F	G	A	B♭	C
C#	D#	E	F#	G#	A#	B	C#
D	E	F	G	A	B	C	D
E♭	F	G♭	A♭	B♭	C	D♭	E♭
E	F#	G	A	B	C#	D	E
F	G	A♭	B♭	C	D	E♭	F
F#	G#	A	B	C#	D#	E	F#
G	A	B♭	C	D	E	F	G
A♭	B♭	C♭	D♭	E♭	F	G♭	A♭
A	B	C	D	E	F#	G	A
B♭	C	D♭	E♭	F	G	A♭	B♭
B	C#	D	E	F#	G#	A	B

Phrygian
Formula: 1 ♭2 ♭3 4 5 ♭6 ♭7 8
Answers:

C	D♭	E♭	F	G	A♭	B♭	C
C#	D	E	F#	G#	A	B	C#
D	E♭	F	G	A	B♭	C	D
E♭	F♭	G♭	A♭	B♭	C♭	D♭	E♭
E	F	G	A	B	C	D	E
F	G♭	A♭	B♭	C	D♭	E♭	F
F#	G	A	B	C#	D	E	F#
G	A♭	B♭	C	D	E♭	F	G
A♭	B♭♭	C♭	D♭	E♭	F♭	G♭	A♭
A	B♭	C	D	E	F	G	A
B♭	C♭	D♭	E♭	F	G♭	A♭	B♭
B	C	D	E	F#	G	A	B

Lydian
Formula: 1 2 3 #4 5 6 7 8
Answers:

C	D	E	F#	G	A	B	C
C#	D#	E#	F𝄪	G#	A#	B#	C#
D	E	F#	G#	A	B	C#	D
E♭	F	G	A	B♭	C	D	E♭
E	F#	G#	A#	B	C#	D#	E
F	G	A	B	C	D	E	F
F#	G#	A#	B#	C#	D#	E#	F#
G	A	B	C#	D	E	F#	G
A♭	B♭	C	D	E♭	F	G	A♭
A	B	C#	D#	E	F#	G#	A
B♭	C	D	E	F	G	A	B♭
B	C#	D#	E#	F#	G#	A#	B

Mixolydian

Formula: 1 2 3 4 5 6 ♭7 8

Answers:

C	D	E	F	G	A	B♭	C
C#	D#	E#	F#	G#	A#	B	C#
D	E	F#	G	A	B	C	D
E♭	F	G	A♭	B♭	C	D♭	E♭
E	F#	G#	A	B	C#	D	E
F	G	A	B♭	C	D	E♭	F
F#	G#	A#	B	C#	D#	E	F#
G	A	B	C	D	E	F	G
A♭	B♭	C	D♭	E♭	F	G♭	A♭
A	B	C#	D	E	F#	G	A
B♭	C	D	E♭	F	G	A♭	B♭
B	C#	D#	E	F#	G#	A	B
F	G	A♭	B♭	C	D♭	E♭	F
F#	G#	A	B	C#	D	E	F#
G	A	B♭	C	D	E♭	F	G
A♭	B♭	C♭	D♭	E♭	F♭	G♭	A♭
A	B	C	D	E	F	G	A
B♭	C	D♭	E♭	F	G♭	A♭	B♭
B	C#	D	E	F#	G	A	B

Aeolian (pure or natural minor):

Formula: 1 2 ♭3 4 5 ♭6 ♭7 8

Answers:

C	D	E♭	F	G	A♭	B♭	C
C#	D#	E	F#	G#	A	B	C#
D	E	F	G	A	B♭	C	D
E♭	F	G♭	A♭	B♭	C♭	D♭	E♭
E	F#	G	A	B	C	D	E

Locrian

Formula: 1 ♭2 ♭3 4 ♭5 ♭6 ♭7 8

Answers:

C	D♭	E♭	F	G♭	A♭	B♭	C
C#	D	E	F#	G	A	B	C#
D	Eb	F	G	A♭	B♭	C	D
E♭	F♭	G♭	A♭	B♭♭	C♭	D♭	E♭
E	F	G	A	B♭	C	D	E
F	G♭	A♭	B♭	C♭	D♭	E♭	F
F#	G	A	B	C	D	E	F#
G	A♭	B♭	C	D♭	E♭	F	G
A♭	B♭♭	C♭	D♭	E♭♭	F♭	G♭	A♭
A	B♭	C	D	E♭	F	G	A
B♭	C♭	D♭	E♭	F♭	G♭	A♭	B♭
B	C	D	E	F	G	A	B

More answer keys…pentatonics, blues, whole tone, whole-half diminished!

Major Pentatonic
Formula: 1 2 3 5 6 8

Answers:

C	D	E	G	A	C
C#	D#	E#	G#	A#	C#
D	E	F#	A	B	D
E♭	F	G	B♭	C	E♭
E	F#	G#	B	C#	E
F	G	A	C	D	F
F#	G#	A#	C#	D#	F#
G	A	B	D	E	G
A♭	B♭	C	E♭	F	A♭
A	B	C#	E	F#	A
B♭	C	D	F	G	B♭
B	C#	D#	F#	G#	B

Minor Pentatonic:
Formula: 1 ♭3 4 5 ♭7 8

Answers:

C	E♭	F	G	B♭	C
C#	E	F#	G#	B	C#
D	F	G	A	C	D
E♭	G♭	A♭	B♭	D♭	E♭
E	G	A	B	D	E
F	A♭	B♭	C	E♭	F
F#	A	B	C#	E	F#
G	B♭	C	D	F	G
A♭	C♭	D♭	E♭	G♭	A♭
A	C	D	E	G	A
B♭	D♭	E♭	F	A♭	B♭
B	D	E	F#	A	B

Diminished (whole-half)
Formula: 1 2 ♭3 4 ♭5 ♭6 ♭♭7 7 8

Answers:

C	D	E♭	F	G♭	A♭	B♭♭	B	C
C#	D#	E	F#	G	A	B♭	B#	C#
D	E	F	G	A♭	B♭	C♭	C#	D
E♭	F	G♭	A♭	B♭♭	C♭	D♭♭	D	E♭
E	F#	G	A	B♭	C	D♭	D#	E
F	G	A♭	B♭	C♭	D♭	E♭♭	E	F
F#	G#	A	B	C	D	E♭	E#	F#
G	A	B♭	C	D♭	E♭	F♭	F#	G
A♭	B♭	C♭	D♭	E♭♭	F♭	G♭♭	G	A♭
A	B	C	D	E♭	F	G♭	G#	A
B♭	C	D♭	E♭	F♭	G♭	A♭♭	A	B♭
B	C#	D	E	F	G	A♭	A#	B

Whole Tone

Formula: 1 2 3 #4 #5 ♭7 8

Answers:

C	D	E	F#	G#	B♭	C
C#	D#	E#	F×	G×	B	C#
D	E	F#	G#	A#	C	D
E♭	F	G	A	B	D♭	E♭
E	F#	G#	A#	B#	D	E
F	G	A	B	C#	E♭	F
F#	G#	A#	B#	C×	E	F#
G	A	B	C#	D#	F	G
A♭	B♭	C	D	E	G♭	A♭
A	B	C#	D#	E#	G	A
B♭	C	D	E	F#	A♭	B♭
B	C#	D#	E#	F×	A	B

Blues Scale

Formula: 1 ♭3 4 #4 5 ♭7 8

Answers:

C	E♭	F	F#	G	B♭	C
C#	E	F#	F×	G#	B	C#
D	F	G	G#	A	C	D
E♭	G♭	A♭	A	B♭	D♭	E♭
E	G	A	A#	B	D	E
F	A♭	B♭	B	C	E♭	F
F#	A	B	B#	C#	E	F#
G	B♭	C	C#	D	F	G
A♭	C♭	D♭	D	E♭	G♭	A♭
A	C	D	D#	E	G	A
B♭	D♭	E♭	E	F	A♭	B♭
B	D	E	E#	F#	A	B

Harmonic Minor

Formula: 1 2 ♭3 4 5 ♭6 7 8

Answers:

C	D	E♭	F	G	A♭	B	C
C#	D#	E	F#	G#	A	B#	C#
D	E	F	G	A	B♭	C#	D
E♭	F	G♭	A♭	B♭	C♭	D	E♭
E	F#	G	A	B	C	D#	E
F	G	A♭	B♭	C	D♭	E	F
F#	G#	A	B	C#	D	E#	F#
G	A	B♭	C	D	E♭	F#	G
A♭	B♭	C♭	D♭	E♭	F♭	G	A♭
A	B	C	D	E	F	G#	A
B♭	C	D♭	E♭	F	G♭	A	B♭
B	C#	D	E	F#	G	A#	B

Melodic Minor (ascending)
Formula: 1 2 ♭3 4 5 6 7 8
Answers:

C	D	E♭	F	G	A	B	C
C♯	D♯	E	F♯	G♯	A♯	B♯	C♯
D	E	F	G	A	B	C♯	D
Eb	F	G♭	A♭	B♭	C	D	E♭
E	F♯	G	A	B	C♯	D♯	E
F	G	A♭	B♭	C	D	E	F
F♯	G♯	A	B	C♯	D♯	E♯	F♯
G	A	B♭	C	D	E	F♯	G
A♭	B♭	C♭	D♭	E♭	F	G	A♭
A	B	C	D	E	F♯	G♯	A
B♭	C	D♭	E♭	F	G	A	B♭
B	C♯	D	E	F♯	G♯	A♯	B

Melodic Minor (descending)
Formula: 8 ♭7 ♭6 5 4 ♭3 2 1
Answers:
Same as Aeolian, only backwards